The Never-Never

For my parents and grandparents
and
In memory of Dr Ken Mills, scholar and friend

The Never-Never
Kathryn Gray

seren

Seren is the book imprint of
Poetry Wales Press Ltd
Nolton Street, Bridgend, Wales, CF31 3BN
www.seren-books.com

ISBN 1-85411-365-8

A CIP record for this title is available from the British Library.

The publisher acknowledges the financial assistance
of the Welsh Books Council.

Printed by Gwasg Dinefwr, Llandybie.

Cover photograph by Lucy Llewellyn

Contents

Then Kilvey Hill, a long adieu
I drag my sorrows hence from you:
Misfortune with imperious sway,
Impels me far from Swansea Bay.

From 'Swansea Bay'
by Ann Julia Hatton ('Ann of Swansea')

Joyrider

Come, hot-wired from the city, down
a one-car lane, over the keystone bridge
that cannot take the headlong rush,
past the parish church where the dead
were married, with your due disregard.

Come, past chrysanthemum baskets
and post office, the adjoining grocer's,
burn the byways, kick up that stereo,
hand fumbling in a glove compartment,
cassette reams spinning out the window.

Come, accelerate forward into pitch
on less than a quarter of a tank left,
as wheels take flight from the ditch,
leave behind the oaks, the sign *Thank you
for driving considerately through our village.*

Come, while those lights come on
within the regularity of their living rooms,
as curtains part, just post-lapsarian,
until now quite unaware that there were
silences, laws observed to be disturbed.

Aim

Your brother would bear down the barrel
of a shotgun intent on blasting our summers,
the force kicking back at his shoulder.
Through his mutters, he could hear it
in the tall grasses and displaced earth
ahead and toward him. For years, the false aim
that went clean through his trainer,
left one toe lopped, was his proof there was life
in those fields. Thinking of him then –
those affected sniper eyes, that hobbled foot,
thumb and finger inched this close to a catch,
how he fell at a single report, was found
one noon by children – how could we have known
that in there, breathing, under those long days,
he'd met himself coming the other way.

The Italians in the Rain

You could almost see them down the backstreets
as it bucketed on a Saturday night, the purr
of a Vespa, his right foot pressed on the kerb,
as he leans over, calls to a girl, and she parleys
a while, then hops on, wraps herself around him.
Or along the sea front, in the mirrors of Sidoli's
where a couple share a Neopolitan with one spoon,
the crest of biscuit between them, fight out
who gets the strawberry and who the chocolate.
You think it's just possible that she always knew
what he'd done with her best friend and sister.
Quicker than the grabbed coat and clipped heels,
from Landore to Y Crwys, now you hear
the parked Fiats as they creak at the beauty spots,
slapped faces and the smashed bottles outside the bars.
And maybe you see there is a man who lifts up
the fryer with its welded batter or does the books
on a stool by the till, the packets of coffee on the shelves
behind him. There's a watercolour of St. Mark's
or the Trevi fountain under the arrow to the toilets,
and as this rain shows no sign of stopping, he looks on
it all, gestures at two passers-by who try the door
a WE ARE CLOSED, returns to his work, forgets
                                        where he is.

Driver

Where exactly on this road it was they dipped
their heads, got in and were driven away
to be back in bed – as they'd said – by eleven,
no witness could remember or agree, but as we go
along at about 70, and you turn the radio up,

I start to think of their laughter, their arms held out,
thumbs straining at the cars that passed them,
the way they might have pushed each other,
swayed, and then a Ford slowed, his face lowered,
he leaned over as the nearside window wound down.

One goes in the front and turns to her friend
again and again, and it could be any other night.
Knitted sleeves rub on the brown leatherette.
Here and there a stray fibre falls. He says nothing,
turns off just before the lights to Jersey Marine.

It is already behind us in the rear-view mirror.
And when we stop, the two of us slam the doors,
watch the boot of your car go around the corner,
it's then things occur: the coiled length of washing
line I saw, a blue sweater I left on the back seat.

The Book of Numbers

The last four digits of your number I can't remember:
the first might be her winning call at bingo,
some of the houses (evens on a street) I never lived in.
A pack of John Player's, then double Mahler's
whatever, the Chanel counter, acrylic sienna daubed
into an earlobe-shaped space on the canvas
or a coin produced from a sleeve, during an evening's
prestidigitation and the deck of incontinent cards
that spills and skims from the croupier's hands.
The times shuffle for each departure gate at Heathrow
or the trains on a station concourse I've memorized
in no particular order, a date for Waterloo, then the buses
tour Trafalgar Square, the total degrees to all those angles,
collapsed roughly to the Equator, tiers becoming slices
of wedding cake; the vital percent off that dress,
without which no man can buy or sell, or else a tetragram,
which brings me back more or less to what I mean,
the last four digits of your number I can't remember.

The Muse, An Estate

You happen now just as the rundown loping alleys
                          or the stairwell descents
of some housing estate (their mapped miscellany
                          of piss, food, sex scent)

happen upon me. Closed and unleverable as that
                          scratched-out, tagged steel
of the month-long broken lifts, in a birl of drum & bass
                          (just to *keep it real*)

or the slatternly toying of the balconied laundry (knickers,
                          bras and boxers)
with all-weather, in hissing naked bulbs and anti-matter
                          there is to the *des res*,

you bend my ear to a desire, these nights, which is
                          unfathomable as concrete,
a ceiling's faceless scream or that fall of you, through me,
                          when you speak.

Alibi

This is what I knew of him: a glass of Dark
held against the mahogany bar, while public parks,
the broad and even lawns of crematoria
thickened at noon; the garden hut's door
which stood ajar (in front, a green deckchair
stretched out and full of sun); a verso stare
in an optic-lined mirror; the benefits
of geranium explicated through the hiss
of my Bitter pulled and frothed to the brim;
that all those years the council never sacked him.
His art was to be in the two places at once.
Back then, for those summer months,
I listened harder than I'd ever done
to good advice *Make it look like you'll come
around the corner any second, everything
casual, like... I always leave a bit of something
behind.* Yes, those lost days crowd into nights
now, when I think of the slump and rise of lights
on the fruit machine, its spiral turn
which seemed interminable, or the quick burn
as a torn-off green swatch of betting slips
in the ashtray caught at an Embassy Filter Tip.
I wonder is it best mid-April or early May
to plant, what (between gulp and drag) he'd say.
Or if this is what I can't or won't see
as I knock my last spare change at an empty
bar: how the grass, on a day like today, will grow,
in a town like the one outside, and know
it's no longer a matter of being here or there
and that, for once, he is not elsewhere.

Friend,

when we find ourselves once more on the floor
of Indian restaurant, public house or pushed back
to cigarette-scarred polyprop seats of taxi rank,
loud and right for the drink we've sunk,
each wrestled down to her quick for past wrongs:
the birthday missed, the boyfriend shared,
skirt returned, but torn, never to be worn again...

when they pull us apart and threaten the police,
and we walk out to a pavement loose with rain,
slivers of kebab meat and our bared toes brace
against the stipples that come heavier, and we are
not together, one a yard ahead of the other, arms
crossed, miles from morning doorsteps, two women
on an A-road and we stop to explain to one another...

please be quiet, come nearer and let our cupped hands
pool the languages of loose change, mascara, fiver.

Where Did Our Love Go?

Record it in the mirror's not-quite-light
of the Ladies like they did:
before the artistic differences,
one of us left, pills, booze, the final split.

Tune out the static from a hairbrush,
sound the clack of the satin-feel make-up
bag to basin, the slap of bra straps
and sigh of a hemline, the smoothed VPL.

Memorise the queue-jarred door stood there
as we elbowed the girls for mascara space,
the backing track it once offered us.
The plaintive we'd yet to understand but still

sang for all we were worth back then,
each of us, as Diana, Mary and Florence.

A Shorter Finish

My love, what we could have used to say that this is
　　　　　　　　　　　　how it was and is:
first, that sweet excess I find to be quite diminished
　　　　　　　　　　　　in my wine glass

as I drink, very carefully, to the last of us, or the
　　　　　　　　　　　　prinked mineral water
brimming, onerous, with its ice in your cradled hand.
　　　　　　　　　　　　Take the laughter

from an adjacent table, for instance; an absolute line
　　　　　　　　　　　　of winter sunlight
that sobers the pavement. And how it was not a matter
　　　　　　　　　　　　of telling night

from day, the day we never met to say whether it was,
　　　　　　　　　　　　in fact, the taste
of wine become water, or water, wine, what was done,
　　　　　　　　　　　　not done, in haste.

Ruskin

It's not meant as design, but accident,
in commentary gone beyond cliché:
a cinematic carrier bag's contents
of dark, ebbed slow-mo down sidroads, say;

market stalls' tarpaulins drawn, the lambent
off-licence doling out its last tonight.
I've walked the terrace rows that are for rent,
run past the lettings to home. And, by rights,

these sheets I pull, now admit myself to,
are cotton-cold in themselves and they know
nothing of available space, through you,
I've filled in, how I'm woken by windows

when every car alarm could be your call.
Lately, even this rain seems personal.

Surrender, Dorothy

It was Dai who'd had the unfortunate habit,
sworn a B&B overrun with *The Singer Midgets*,
who knew something he couldn't say for certain
from behind the puke-spat shower curtain.

This was me, in the next room, playing dead
through shut-eye, wallpaper hung above me in red
patches of eczema loosely passing for flowers,
and later that headboard knocking was ours.

(But say now, at whose heels went those bones,
in the early hours, headed for home?)

Next day we trawled all Splott for a parlour
and picked it out like a ring: the perfect weather
that in dreams he'd made of my left thigh,
the message piped in cloud across a cloudless sky.

Garage

All pasts must be put somewhere: the apt kind of nail,
a nut or bolt, then the screwdriver you'd forgotten
you were never looking for; an entire iconography
of Woolworth's stars and slovenly angels; the perambulator's
hood and the off-cuts of bathroom tiles pickled,
in their half-light, near a shut and unhummed freezer still
believing in Sunday joints or the iron ice-pops lifted
one summer by a child's clammy fist. Here, simple Dulux,
petrified in a virgin tin, holds the sum untried hope
of newlywed, first-time buyers and, in the box,
merely happened upon, a loose swatch of Anaglypta
is a lounge, as was, a decade gone, whose print I read,
like the tabloid around that lampshade, as a *then* politics;
while, against brick, the Raleigh outgrows again stabilisers
and its pedals recall a girl in a *no hands* freewheeling
along some slope of road. You are the repercussive error
and outwear I enter now only to add to, in a documentary
too intimate for landfill or skip, the dumb-down
too artless and uncensored for an attic's precious retrospect,
where, with an ancient clink/clink of the Braille necks
of Dandelion & Burdock empties, the pop-man may,
by chance, slow up this ordinary cul-de-sac again, his van
in a corona of an afternoon much like this one, and the queue
assembles for 10p returns long since scrapped as tender.

Omertá

And so it happens you go back to Sicily in your mind,
as you must (of an evening and without the typical kind
of warning), to shoot the bastard who killed your father
and your brother to end the sorry line, *alla* Don Corleone,
with the pistol in your hand, as you run to off-by-heart hills,
weighing heavy as those three hemispheres of ice cream
that slip and fall to sag and unfold in their stainless steel
banana-split boat. For every man must chance to dream
of what he never did, stood doing simply what he always did.

And here is the Tiger Bay as was, with the steam and silt
bitter as espresso, this part of a city's air before it tasted
of Amaretto, while the dockland development's lights blink
in rain, asylum, melancholia, and a high counter's mahogany
is some scene straight out of a Coppola in your busied
                                                    parlour.
These walls bear witness how, of all things, you survived:
each christening, with its fancy, lugubrious Catholicism,
of your progeny, the progeny of men you since forget,
and neatly framed, as if it was always the matter of destiny.

And as if from the old country, your wife's stockings hiss
past chairs, their static is the dust road of any of its summers;
her lips a passionate innocence of the synch and segue,
the nervous complications as shorthand scrawls the order.
Blood's pared to a pinprick through Welsh daughter-in-laws,
but you are returning now in the first language to vendetta –
for your son's sons, their fair-skinned sons – as your fingers
grip around the trigger and pull to sunder the same landscape
as that place in the mountains after which you were named.

Nostalgia

If I could tell now of just how that grass felt –
itchy, summer wet – as we rolled the incline,
raced each other down, bad-landed in a heap;

if I could pull from my pocket the chalk dust
from shattered *Parma Violets* and blow this
from my palm like so, then I'd be getting

some proximity toward his hand spanned up
my skirt and that particular instant, loosed
and everywhere as pollen, when my eyes filled.

Meteorology

And, passing through only, it was then I thought of you,
how once you'd said it was that I opened up to you
as a cleft in the clouds can speak of a heat, a dry spell,
as a tumble of nimbostratus can come at us from a slouch
of any horizon. And I thought of that very afternoon,
terraced gardens strung with the swings of pegged lines,
which were, in fact, the isobars on which the *smalls*
of our lives were hung; and then it was I saw, here
and there, the woman with the basket, pulling down
each of the ephemera, a damp cotton corner of bedsheet,
while tarpaulins were drawn across a court in Wimbledon.
And then light occurred, as if an idea, over someone's
kitchen lino. I thought of telegraph wires running
relays from county to county in a slip and grip of hands,
while a motorway sped and brought to us an onwards,
a loss, an everything everywhere as weather, and I looked
out to a lopped half of sun dropped upon an arable land,
before returning again to where the convex rain held
steady the tremens of the window and, for the moment,
there was a yard, tilted right hip, a woman with a basket.

Bethesda

And the House of God? Over there,
with its all-but-one-window put out;

a nineteenth century-come-spraycanned
fucks and *Rhian loves*. My people

swore that it was built in steel and drink.
But they were wrong. It's made of glass,

a hew of stone to brick, an unlearning
of language that speaks no praise or pity.

Even local kids no longer stop and stare
over judders of their handlebars

as they press on to their past and fast.
They can't know what they've missed.

Nobody tells them that this is the address,
that the dead are what will outlive us.

The Continents

You've come to know well by now these letters, doorstepped
and sworn by heart, but never written, then the receiver clutched,
hung-up – this long-distance expense being all said and done.

So – as you'll never have to attempt to name that voice in one,
skim pages to a shaky sign-off, return before you get the plot –
here's a word in the ear or cupped in a hand that's yours or mine.

Remember? Both stunted, we've laboured over this experiment
before, to find for our efforts – as we took five paces apart –
that we were stuck fast in that same glitch of disquietude I feel

whenever I open scissors with meticulous concern and measure
or dig out the last from the Ski Yoghurt pot: a something coming
upwards through a biro tip's puncture, across along the taut string.

The King's Head

Now I well know that I am not the first to liken the two:
this beered-up, close air being ancient, having a sacrosanct
and ceremony of light and dark, the font or the missal;
but whatever it may be that leads the cellar, barrels, pricelist
and tap onward in the fear of God, began with you.
So let us now avoid the rush, the Scampi, a filled baguette,
and the rite, near-extinction of the Ploughman's Lunch
across this country's counties. Three is the empty hour:
baskets tinking the bells of glasses and, here, the back-breaker
pew – the only one that will do – where the stained pane
falls in a flush over beer mats, the stick and scuff of table.
Are we two not, in fact, the true devout, bearing as we do
our clammy witness to the dartboard's years of patient
stigmata, our pores breaking out in sympathy for its cork?
What need have we of an iconography? If so, what better
than these as its sum: the welling tear of a vodka optic,
those Marys in relief behind the bar, their bored, open faces,
readied hands, our proof of a *caritas*, if any, in this world?
I well know I am not the first to weigh up a parity;
was it not yourself who once intoned *This place is a church:*
I, its humble minister, you, my sorry flock? And so let us be
seated to take in what, to some, could pass as the after-life,
though we have declared this a personal genesis –
the slow business of these hours, oh pastor, father, publican –
before an evening or a morning have found their division,
before the waters are folded back, an earth and a quease
return to haunt and hold us. Here, you could walk from
a stink of the Gents, rearranging yourself like the plausibly
risen again, and I would take it on faith: the cigarette-cough
laugh hacking over my concern and question, the stubbed-out
break, like your place, where there settles this draught.

If Souls

If I was the eldest son who'd pressed his mouth
against the wings' beat, last left of your lungs

and let it fill his own, limp to take its place among
the stinking annals of the air, the truth

a nightly recreation in someone's back garden;
say its mass was less than birds' breath, a fall of hair

or the space between the hands and prayer,
all that we can't measure held by the rapt men

stood for the photo-finish from whose split lips
would come this tear, a little flutter of betting slips –

Katie Parker

The queue at The Principality smelt of a life somehow:
Embassy Number 1, a spritz of Mornay Eau de Toilette –
in Lavender, I think – fitted kitchens, a bin liner, children.
And that winter's day I held our life, its hot deposit,
between the palms of my leather-gloved hands.
So my mind turned from Abertawe to dearthed Iowa;
so the tenners in the Manilla may have passed
for a fat gun along the crease and fold.
The licked-thumb count went on methodical
behind the glass like some peculiar penance. I watched
our gains go, the black blind suddenly coming down.
And it was then that I ran, love – but now from nothing –
to a car ticking over on the double-yellow like memory,
a hand squeezing mine, the cumulus across my eyes,
which held a glimpse of the V8, futurist, in a Debenham's
shop-front as we pulled off, remembering your lips parted
slack to a mouth rich and dark as the last field of loam
tyres had once sent out in wheels against the close air.
Forgive me only for what I did not do. I wanted a home.

On Skorpios

And when I think of Jackie Onassis,
her fingers tugging sand on Skorpios

as a wave all but carries her legs out;
her recomposure, lead-heavy bouffant

coasted by the *sunkissed zephyrs of a cove*;
Ari kneeling as he cups the word *love*

(and both, for a moment, can believe it);
it's the docked *Christina*, where a girl sits

or sat, her curled toes dangled over, I see.
And, of course, this is the stuff of biography:

the honeymooners, the annular reef
of that island and the white handkerchief

like a flag, in a back seat through Paris,
raised to the pallor of Maria Callas.

Assignation

Strangers come and go and come, and true, we only just hear them
through these walls – but enough – as they've heard us by the hour,
while a typical afternoon's light falls half-hearted on a corded kettle,
thimbles of milk, the crisp sachets of sugar, the PG Tips, Nescafé.

It's what we've done with time, not wanting to be that much alone
(or so it goes), and I've filled in each moan, the intervals between
conversation, stung by the heat of their drawn-curtain futures
and uniform fumble for the alias and explanation. *It's not me, it's you.*

But they're not us, you've said, pressed the point so many times
I repeat it in your absence like a joint signature we might have penned
elsewhere, but then we didn't; everything being settled in advance
and cash, the faux-leather reception register's long become defunct.

But whenever it is that we walk the familiar, bald-carpeted corridors,
curled from the chipped skirting, appalled by their own frank horror,
and on whichever floor, it's fear keeps my head down, moves me fast,
in case my love and I were to find ourselves in the arms of another.

You Hated Your Flat

Your flat frightened you. Your flat
Where I felt at home. The strip-light,
Your face in the mirrors, the soft pine
Furnish and finish to everything, frightened you.
Your schooling had somehow neglected your flat:
The gas grill, domestic science and the boiler's drum.
You did not have the books, your mind was closed
To the signs and the 80 watts of migraine light
Made your eyeballs burr. Bosch
Held out a drill and you took it
To alcoves, a born-blonde and bred Suttonite.
You saw right down through the spirit level's bubble
And recognized yourself in it, stepped back
To a world lopsided as your smile, your books
Sliding west towards the student halls of Bristol.
So we sat as tourists on the edge of the bathtub
Watching the blocked pipe simply reach on up,
The grey-faced of Dyno-Rod bent over sewers,
Straightening up their rubber gloves and going in;
A wheeze of methane had you over the bowl.
The unexpected cost that hid itself inside the walls,
The crack of inspiration that travelled across the ceiling
What was waiting for you. Your flat
Was the landscape of a nightmare, the builder's dust covers
You slept for weeks with, the sink's amputation
No year of VSO could have glamorised.
What Rentokil scrabbled for under an off-cut of carpet.
Your flat was what you tried to wake up from
And could not. I see you, in that moonlight,
Walking the empty pavements of Putney,
The single life waiting for a taxi,
A city girl, still not understanding.
Thinking you still hold the deposit
In the happy world, your father's guarantee.
Happy, and your new flat still to be found.

The Wardrobe

This wood is not about the old wives and the oak
or the ash that separates a summer from a soak.

And that afternoon when a sky turned dark,
though it might have been the ark

itself as twelve men in Sunday drink had shouldered it
from the house of the last widow left

on Beaufort Hill, this is not about the front step,
the angle, lift and give, the driving curses of their stoops;

not even how, at a loss, they took at it with the axe
and nailed it by bits back; every loving cuff and coax.

Or how for years the doors would fall open,
as if it was – loosely speaking – a lopsided heaven;

how it proved by the burning it was only wood,
as much this felled as when it stood.

And last, with every man now decades gone,
singing, I push them down the Taff to Avalon,

the river become rain or a spread of that fire.
No. These are the stories. This was the weather.

"These Things I Carry"

after Darinka Rumistrewicz

Imagine the suitcase I carry bearing hard west,
inside it, all these things I've left:

the village tongue, a tic, the local shrug
or the must of the rolled-up rug

stitched with the light as it fell in a hall
and a kicked-over bucket, fresh from a well

that makes of the grass a network of rivers,
crossing which I learned the balance of these

things I carry with me, each unmourned,
unable either to keep or return.

The Cwtch

Here's a word for us – strictly untranslatable –
having nothing of the kick of legs and stone as Babel
falls (and because of which you'd never hear in chapel)

from the softer tongue of a woman
who birthed to the world working men,
well-travelled down to black, carrying her pain

upwards in their arms, which unfold,
really, never, but keep close that old
word at picket lines, in conversation with the cold,

which some say is "a place for coal, under the stairs"
or this very bundle here, which we'll bear
along with us on the way to where.

Guilt

It can seem like history, ad hoc, Imperial Leather
lathered away to the gold leaf sticker,
the coal tar smoke through a fist of water.

In a B&B in Colwyn Bay you wake to find the old brand
and feel morning spread from sea to land
or think of your father from nowhere, understand

how a workday morning for years was little more
than the end-of-terrace billboard's just post-war
Lifebuoy carp of *down there, behind the ears,*

Now Wash Your Hands in the raw. The filth
of an inside-collar Saturdays at dances. The *Macbeth*
you read when you were twelve. Hold your breath.

You spell out that word against a mirror. *Cunt.*
Remember how she gave you a clout,
dragged you to the basin to clean your mouth out?

We're better than that, you cant as of old; the Lux
slapped against the beige flannel, the knucks
she lathered up babbling to the Armitage Shanks.

The Light Factory

Tippy-toed, love, there you were, holding up
the Osram 60w to bayonet that gap

between your small hand and the gone light,
the kind that makes us dizzy for the heights.

You see, one window was seeing stars,
and further back to our phosphor

selves through a box, upside-down on a wall
in the dark room, our outline the caul

of what we were for before we were born.
I'd swear now it was you up there who'd said *Creation*

makes us more alone and *in all serious-*
ness and *art teaches you that* and so on, *thus.*

But what to make of it, your aim being true;
your hand moved, the hand that moves about you.

Recess

The way light will fill and form this very office
that you see just now close in on you, as it is, left

to Whitehall's forgotten months, the minister's desk
brings back the sadness of the civil servant:

England happening somewhere down an avenue,
summers no more than a fountain pen, a *billet doux*

quite unbegun on the bed of a floral room,
hot as shame behind the sulks of a teenage girl.

And for a moment the Whitaker's Almanac holds
what she held to her breast by the library doors,

all the sweetest delineations of knee to ankle
you found yourself sketching in the English Finals:

one among the many islands. Vicissitudes
in the study, your father's awkwardness in the face

of the window at noon, commend the sea air
at Brighton; the sand she never kicked behind her

beats a path to which everything under the sun is cast –
from sandwiches to the minor past – and falls away

as light unpacks the world and the years of water
swallow your gaze to take in the splay of her toes.

History, 1984

Row by row, the desks can still tell us how it was:
under each, the thumb-press of gum gone to bone
as we open our books at *Chapter 1, Tollund Man*,

and Anne-Marie stammers the length of the line
A m-man p-possibly a v-v-victim of so-som -me c-crime,
and the words are wet flecks of peat as picked off

by the gloved and studied hands of archaeologists
to reveal in the hollowed eye-sockets an evidence,
which will leave a boy at the back none the wiser

and nails scoring away at his scalp lifts of dandruff;
a traffic on an easy passage to the window's light
until its hang will fall below and sift to out of sight.

This was our present: those doodles of marginalia
for U2, The Cure; a feint our notes slipped under
on the slopes of our penmanship, bearing witness

to our disgrace. Even then, on palms, meant to last,
those makeshift tattoos by the Bic and the compass
were fading to the newsprint of scabs in the valleys,

of Libya, Yvonne Fletcher, Marvin Gaye *shot dead*
by his own father, and the desks shook with history
or *th-e r-r-ritual bu-u-rial of p-p-primitive so-s-society.*

The Storm

after Ingeborg Bachmann

What to say of that evening, except there was a path
we walked, which made a stunted avenue of the bushes,
and the sky above us, a meticulous traffic, gathered up
until it seemed huddled to the folds of those same roses.

What, but footfalls ahead; the argument swithering air
to a black weather, while leaves caught the light's edge
like razors, to hold and shake the wake of a thunderclap,
by which we counted out the seconds to this distance.

Mount Lee

"So on that terrible night in September 1932, Peg announced to her Uncle Harold that she was going to take a walk. She was last seen alive heading down Beachwood Canyon toward Mount Lee."

"Peg Entwhistle" from *Haunted Hollywood* by Troy Taylor

Come, my girl, with your tripping heels a path
unto the row of empty stalls unseated off Broadway
and, further, to the orange groves of California;
tipping each stockinged toe at the rungs of a ladder,
the bang of your baby blonde fallen down
over blue eyes still lit up even at this hour of night;
no, with neither the head nor feet for heights.

Sweet somnambulant! Pause, and become again
the climbing lilt of gardenia dabbed at a throat,
be the hem of the best dress snagged at bushes,
away as a signature, the sealing of envelopes
and the lag, a sense somehow of being late or lost;
the moment your calling first entered air,
a fizz and blow of a bulb as you dropped from the *H*.

A Return to Love in Ludlow

There, the nosegay's wilt on that table rain-shadowed
by the window offers proof, so many end-of-summers on,

that, once, two shared the piano stool and pounded out
Chopsticks, as cherry pith was stamped to ink the length

of the lane you're walking through the splashy evenings
now, the textbook Manilius – a page nipped back at *Notes* –

bursting from your coat pocket, and, where, you imagine
the underlined exclamations stroked in bold at a margin

happen like sudden laughter, yes, laughter at the ear
of a lover, and in the woods all the boys hanged long since.

The Field

Let's say that first day you were nailing
a mirror to a tree or – even – nailing a tree
to a mirror, in a little corner of England,
with the birds peep-peep-ing
and tinny above you and going absolutely
nowhere, like the old lie which makes
all the difference between this and that
twenty years ago but before you – see? –
you have your own hands. You have a gun
and catch a glimpse of the streams of tent
as the razor sinks. *Christ.* Remember
how they took a clothes peg, drew
a cross at your throat, threatened
to dig your voice out with it? By the third day
each bird's pegged to the fence,
the Calor's gone, the only sound's the kettle's
long thrown whistle to a river,
the space that lives inside the mirror's
lightning bolt. The last lamb's bleats
are broken by the *down* and *down* of a stone.
Only now can you properly begin,
your face cut to shit, your boss eye snooking
to the hills, the only safe place left.

The Singularity

Through their silent field of radiation, the waves were emitted,
though, of course, we could never see them, only the observable
tics of REM am/pm, always afterwards, you would live within.

Perfectly round and beyond this, something grew – as if
                                                    planned for –
even as a cultured pearl and, more, simply kept growing there,
until each of our days fell into one another and the space fell out.

I consider an eyelid lifted, propped by a finger, recall the blue iris
lost in a trauma of light as they examined you. The rays thinned
and lengthened infinitely as you went, and it was then I thought

of gravity, the proximity of any star, now swollen, now collapsible –
safely far along the wash, the arms of our system – as rudimentary
documentaries for the layman pragmatically assure me. And how,

in their wake, there's only the matter, taken and honed to a point,
post-event's horizon, of nothing, and inside, as we move, more of it.

A Drop

Dangled from a bridge by Mark and Morgan,
this was the oft-remembered summer idyll:
the tongues of his pockets hanging limp,
a living river's stink of dead bodies; the beyond still
of its surface like the weathered sky above:
a black, refusing to give anything up.

Even now, he could find himself counting
each loss as it swooned past or bombed: football
stickers, a pack of Chewitts; the dinky New Testament
handed out in assembly that morning;
the paper scraps, on which would certainly be written
O.K., a muscled cartoon heart and, under, Eluned's
signature skittering along a hankie; his glasses, lately gone,
as a penny plocks through water; the blood to his skull
flooding his one, good eye to a thrum of red;
the world come impossibly full.

At times, if he chanced to think, his mouth
gave itself up again to that old thirst;
one foot, then the other, would lift from
a sweat of his decades long-lost trainers;
below, the two on the bridge who carried him
this far were an endless drop he entered
and broke, head first.
He was young.

These are the prices you pay for love.

Secondhand

Come in from the filthy, dated rain, I tiptoe the shelf
along and mouth the inventory across like a lifetime of loss:
The Third Man, The Rainbow, and – less than

a breath's gutter – pull out this classic, nipped back
halfway through, *Treasure Island Complete and Unabridged,*
before it drops. Yes, I can almost see your flounder now,

my sweet, in your schoolcoat, sopping; your fingers
streaking the spines, upstairs, in that little place just off
Duke Street, calling itself a bookshop, biding the while

for the girl to go and make a brew, leaving to you a pass
to lope the spiral case downwards to the Dutch mags,
palming out the lone fiver to the bloke who stank of mint,

brownpaper, something else. Of course, she never
went, you bottled it; without warning, somehow found
yourself slipping *The Girl Guide Handbook* nightly under covers,

thrapping your itch to those girly reef knots and bandages;
shoving it under the bed. *Crap.* So I turn back to Saturdays,
your mother out, the *Freemans Catalogue* pgs.108-9,

the static bridge as the sheen ripped apart on your lap.
I imagine you there and – to help things along – Morgan's
boast of how in the library, at lunchtime, he'd got it out

for the lovely Anne-Marie, her eyebrows meeting in query,
and there you are with the picture of his small cock lost
in his fist, as he goes for it here/there, not knowing where

he began, his bite-backs hirpling down the aisle of quiet,
his dad's stash shuddering the mind with its memory;
the tits and clit, the undone fly; and how the dinner table

came to fall so silent evenings, and no-one, especially you,
wanting to ask or know how it was that Baden-Powell's
little blue bible ever came to find itself on your top shelf.

For a Foot

Not the goose-step of childhood callipers
or the snot-drunk tears of fathers,
but a foot, never without a boot; an uplift
and steel that evened your black horizon out.
What happens at the bare knuckle
of life or the S-bend of an ankle
all legend now: the night you levelled
Bryn Bastard in the snug, almost killed
some cunt for calling you a cripple.
A lament being really this simple,
that what I miss is permanent winter
as snowfall sculpted under flaking leather,
which apes me into limps and sumps
of someone else's century, your stump.

Dettol Stings

Before you know it, you're walking the appointed corridor,
a dark vinegar or urine colour and, of course, there's the bucket
left outside 3B; inside it, noises, a canon of playing field voices.
From nowhere, schoolyard concrete rises up to meet your fall

and as a ball careers down a verge and a girl chalks numbers
at the paving, a stone is thrown, tears, and you follow through
to the same room, bleeding as if it were not all years before,
where she will turn to you, a studied look of *What's the matter*

(you forget she died of cancer) and now, from the wad, balls
a squeak of cotton wool between her thumb and finger. Still, you
can't say where it hurts, but here is your knee, a pomegranate
red in the yellow, the ball pressed to the mouth of the bottle,

and the gulp, as always, will fill the seat of a chair at the back
of a class and drip to a spread of hot piss across the polymer floor.
Once more, you choke on flecks of black, stones scoured
to chalk, feel stings enter the open; the high window's flung

out somewhere, someone calls; an Elastoplast snags and snaps
away from a scab and, for that lag, it might easily be summer,
but there happens again a sharp stink of something, not flowers,
and the corridor stops running now. You stand before the door.

Localised

Mother, what we know of each other is mainly a weather,
so days when I say *mainly fine, some cloud here and there,*
you might pause on the line. *It's bucketing down.*

But, sometimes, there falls hard now between us
the very first drop which cannot break but spreads a silence
we share, being really that shape, precisely the colourless.

Spray

He could swear the silence was for a single moment
such as this, when a girl would chance to shirr a little
at her wrist, coming within his earshot the coast
of sand and shingle from less than a mile away now,

as the car whips past grasses grown taller than him,
his mother's lips turn to mouth again the words
to a song gone off the tongue, while the first ever sea
he can see bobs from the leatherette of a seat, 1963,

pulling him back, as his father swerves the cliff-road
down, its line looped on and on like a signature, to
the laughter as the road putters out just here, an elbow
making farcical billows of a ham-fisted deck chair

and, even later, as he watched her wade in, wrists
waving the water and salt-flecked air and reaching out
for his hands, the space between the rush and break.
He could swear the silence was for a single moment.

The Watch

But for you, I would have walked blind through
the analogue of this entire world:
the stared-out of a doctor's waiting room,
lip-read ticks next to velour coastal shelves
of nine carat wedding rings, the golden charms
our kind of life anticipates. Be assured:
the circumscription of a day
would have passed me by in the slant
and slop of a window cleaner's humble,
sun-filled bucket, with no hour found
and broadly sounded above the rain-striated
edifices of the townhalls and libraries built
by the good men of the continental cities, where I have
stood, waited as the last rang itself to dead.

No, with you was where it started, long after love
had invented it in a bedroom in '72.
Remember. How you bought it? The fancy wheel
of numerals, the pearl face of emptiness?
The two hands that moved to steady this?
How, when you asked, I couldn't say, because
by now it was '84, a brave new world of Casio?

Do not underestimate the diagrammatical sweeps
you made. I see them move at a thumb's flick
of consecutive pages like primitive cartoons.
Truly, it was logic that night that fell between us,
the genius that regarded the adumbrated earth,
brought sophistication to the sun-dial.

Years later, Einstein's parable, doled out by
the din of clapped desks, the Physics lesson,
would render all moments from then to this
a matter for light and position, a train pulling
away from a pre-war platform. But it was you
who gave me the watch, as under a late lamp it still
goes as if to prove time and darkness equable.
The more I have, the more I lose.

Or Nothing

after William Carlos Williams

Or nothing,
a pious wish to whiteness gone over,
a cluster, flower by flower,
white desire, empty, a single stem,
until the whole field is a
stem one by one, each to its end,
to which the fibres of her being
is a blossom under his touch,
a tiny purple blemish, each part.
His hand has lain there, is
of her whiteness, wherever
each flower is a hand's span
at the center of each flower,
white as can be, with a purple mole.
Here is no question of. Whiteness
does not raise above it.
The field by force, the grass
of the wild carrot taking
so remote a thing. It is a field,
anemone petals. Nor so smooth, nor
her body is not so white as –

Hereafter

for Doug Williams, wherever

You make not even anecdote by this uncertain light,
such curtain-filtered afternoons of drink and family rite
where we might praise the good or those of good intent,
who made of life much less than they had meant.

On cancer wards they slept through kids and wives
to dream of nurses and other people's lives,
solving this was how a private eternity
is made and found (the last of love hardens to dignity

for mugs who never asked for more or spivving
with the fancy-piece, though some might call *that* a living).
But you will survive us all, you unaccounted-for,
and hard to tell how much is absence or is awe

that you have gone beyond what burial can allow,
become a silence after bombs, snow.

The Collect

How they must come as if we'd planned them,
through school days and the scraps of afternoon
that whip the echoics of estates,
and laying all the old myths to waste:

Never & Son, who by the heat of burnt-out tyres
go about the briefcase of an altogether human business.
As if it were writ years ago with a stick
in the kids' canal or in the everywhere of stink

we make of factories, curtains would be drawn,
nothing would move but that scrag of lawn,
the curling putter of a ball, this catalogue's
ebbing polythene and uplifted tawny leg of a dog

against a wall. That when they'd come
we, all grown-up now, would never be home.

The Pocket Anglo-Welsh Canon

One day, you and I will walk the aisles of libraries,
with their plausible stink of the shut generations,
to pass over an entire canon that's long been thumbed
to stub and take from some or other imagined shelf
the intimate apocrypha.
                              Cloth binding
will be the opened-out in prayer, the warp of weather
down the stone and across denominations, where air
is more than lost, gone a pointillism of coal dust. I mean
the cant of the great and good who never made us famous,
and in the first language, namely *English*. And I swear
that though these words were never ours,
they will have happened like a history, share that taste
of copper on the tongue, have a certain easiness
with human heat; they'll be the pure that's cast
by men in ballots, a pickling of steel.
How the negative was to right the light from dark,
the schoolroom's slag-flood glare will wake dead arms.
This, the book we hold and in our hands.

An Epic

One thing I know: it begins in the "home of mist",
this, my family's chronicles,
with the hawk's deep regard sole sorrow resident
to my mother's fortnight-long confinement.

The bawling, bastard version down the cream-peel corridors
of Caerphilly Miners'
Hospital, a midwife's near-miss. The certain wrack
in the torso's strick

of eczema for months she fretted
over. As in the – *Ms.*, days of love and bliss and callow debt,
of working nights and down for ore.
How she held me then, true blight and hoard,

in the throes of what, as likely as not, is a *tarnkappe*
falling lightly to a shimmy of the river in her lap.

Saint Anthony of Padua

My only saint, O hear now the prayer of raw knees,
of dowsing palms under brown settees,
all commonplaces of fivers, keys and things misplaced,
itching back to their anonymities. I call upon the grace

of faces pasted to pissed-up walls of the coach stations,
your cult of tired tourists moved just clear of salvation
and geriatrics dribbling for the name of their daughter,
the flare's phosphor bronze over that body of water.

Not even a clock, the sameness of and unused days
can trouble or escape the kind tragedy of your gaze.
And when I miss and drop like this, I'll prove you near
to the soul and the sock, my sad career.

A Voyeur's Volume

A jaundiced Harold Robbins or Jackie Collins
you might hold on a balcony, the remnants
of previous occupants, like us, on the two-week,
no-see package; the way you might pronounce
svelte, draw it out to the tip of your tongue,
to where your foot might then reach along,
lift up my sarong, and it is quiet in the passage
of villas that runs on down below us. *Thigh*,
you say, your leg drawn back, and turn
to another page that's well lined at the spine,
smiling to yourself and no one in particular.

The Prodigal

My friends, we came to put this town in its place,
to leave the hard-faced
local hills to blunt the sun and render their rain.
We are above any blame.

The track ahead is spent matchsticks,
our widowed mothers crying over the hob, a pub trick.

How many times have we gone to never return?
But it can be told only once in the one tongue.

Note

'These Things I Carry'(pg. 34)

Darinka Rumistrewicz was born in Krakow in 1890. Landing alone on Ellis Island in 1910, she settled in Brooklyn where she carried out a number of menial jobs before marrying a second-generation Polish carpenter, Stefan Notkoff, in 1912. After the death of their only child Katerina in 1915, they parted, and Darinka set to work on *Za Chlebem* ('For Bread'), a moving prose-poetry account of the economic and personal struggles of the Polish in America in the early twentieth century. *Za Chlebem* was published under the pen name Karol Rosen by W.D. Rechtzeit in 1920 to some acclaim and popularity within the Polish community. After 1925, Darinka left Brooklyn, and no record of her after this period can be traced. She remains in death, as in life, an elusive and enigmatic émigré.

Acknowledgements

Acknowledgements are due to the editors of the following publications where some of these poems first appeared: *Agenda, Anvil New Poets 3 (Anvil, 2001), The Times Literary Supplement, Poetry Review, Poetry Wales, Stand, New Welsh Review* and *Rising*.

'Recess' first appeared on BBCi.

I am grateful to The Society of Authors for an Eric Gregory Award in 2001.

I would like to express my gratitude to Michael Donaghy, Roddy Lumsden and John Stammers for their early support, encouragement and friendship, and to Amy, my enthusiastic editor at Seren. Thanks, too, go to Christian, Celia, Cam, Gerry and, most especially, the 'Swansea Girls', who have provided me with so much raw material.

Lastly, I thank Andrew Neilson, unstinting critic of the work and the woman, to whom I find myself most happily indebted.